SPIRITUAL CONCEPTS

A VISUAL REPRESENTATION

GABRIELA CASINEANU

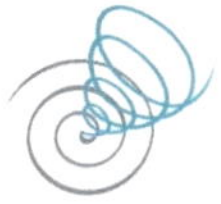

Images/Concept/Cover Design/Formatting: Gabriela Casineanu

Editing: Christina Friend-Johnston

Library and Archives Canada Cataloguing in Publication

Casineanu, Gabriela, 1961—, author

Spiritual Concepts: A Visual Representation, 1st ed.

ISBN: 978-1-989948-02-6 (paperback)

ISBN: 978-1-989948-04-0 (hardcover)

ISBN: 978-1-989948-03-3 (ebook)

PRAISE FOR THIS BOOK

A spiritual journey in few pages. Beautiful story and inspiring pictures. Intriguing and asking for more exploration.
    ~ I.B.

Beautiful and powerful healing work integrating soul/spirit and art. Uplifting!
    ~ T.N.

Stunning paintings, very meaningful and very transformational for me. I received healing from many of them.
    ~ L.R.

Amazing paintings and inspiration! The artist's true essence manifested in these paintings.
    ~ A.H.

DISCLAIMER

The information and resources in this book are provided for informational and educational purposes.

Neither the author nor the publisher can be held responsible for the use of the information provided within this book.

CONTENTS

VIBRATIONS

EPIGRAPH

Spiritual development gives rise to mental happiness.

~ The Dalai Lama

INTUITIVE PAINTING FOR VISUAL REPRESENTATIONS

Did the adults encourage you to follow your passion when you were a child?

I enjoyed drawing in elementary school, but an exigent art teacher discouraged me: "Ten (the maximum grade) is only for the teacher," he used to say. I never understood why; he wasn't a student like us, why would he expect a child's drawings to be at a teacher level? I've got only one 10 in four years: "That's good," he said, "you've added some shadows." He never taught us to add shadows! Although other people liked my drawings, his harsh critique affected my confidence. I was a very sensitive child, not knowing how to handle such situations. So I stopped drawing, thus turning off my creative expression without realizing it.

Years later, a French friend invited me to visit Giverny, France, to see Monet's house and gardens. Amazed by the beauty of that place on a beautiful spring day, I said to my friend "if you've never been a painter, you become one if you live here!" The myriad of colourful flowers that garnered those gardens, the famous pond that made it in Monet's paintings, were so inspiring! That place deeply touched me, a brief flicker rekindling in my soul. I barely noticed it and left it there. "Who am I to paint? I never took painting classes!"

Little did I know that my creative side was not meant to be ignored. In 2007, a friend offered me a free ticket to join her on a two-day experiential workshop in Chicago. I was already into coaching by then, after leaving my technical background behind, so it was tempting.

Life taught me to look for and follow signs when I need to make a decision. I refused the ticket at first, then two weeks later she mentioned it again. "That seems to be a sign," I thought. And so we drove nine hours to Chicago… to what became a turning point in my life!

The coaching training and experience already gave me a glimpse into a world that I never envisioned before, which fascinated me. This workshop though, and the following ones, hooked me to dive in at a deeper level… opening me up to a spiritual path.

For someone like me—a logical engineer who learned nothing about religion or spirituality while growing up in Romania— that was quite a shift!

A particular session from those self-growth workshops—we were told it was Holotropic Breathwork®—became a transformative experience, which opened a healing gate for me… and unleashed my creativity! At the end of that session I was drawing with ease sacred geometrical shapes (which didn't happen before), while using both hands in parallel. I never used my left hand for drawing prior to that experience! And a powerful energy was flowing through my body. Although I was tired after that session, back into the hotel room I continued to draw until late hours into the night… and the weeks that followed. This experience also reignited my willingness to paint, feeling no fear or "Who am I…?" this time. Talking with other participants, I realized that each of us had a unique experience with that session, which is normal from what I've read.

Back home, it didn't take long for me to buy paint, brushes and canvases. However, I soon realized that using a brush was restricting… so I started to paint with my fingers, curious to discover what images their movements would bring forth. It was so freeing!

Since I was learning spiritual concepts that were hard to grasp, I became curious about what could be their visual representation. For each painting, I started with a word in mind, intuitively picked the paint colours, entered a quasi-meditative state, and surrendered to my finger movements to bring forth an image from the *unknown*. It was just that! No thinking, no judging, not imposing any idea or perception. What I found funny: my fingers already knew when to stop, like they knew when I'd finished a painting. A little later, I took time to meditate on each painting, and you'll read in this book the insights I've got.

When I was sick with a flu… I painted *Healthy*—it made me feel a bit better each time I looked at it, until I regained my health.

When I couldn't talk… I painted *Before Opening Up*— curious to see the visual expression of the frustration I was accumulating inside. Then, when my voice came back, I painted *After* —which surprised me how well it represented my state of mind at that point.

Feeling trapped in a situation made me create *Freedom*—a painting representing the feeling to hold on until I broke through.

After hiking the Old Inca Trail to Machu Picchu I painted *Beyond*—curious about the meaning of that experience.

When I look at any of my paintings, I pay less attention to the visual aspect… and more to how it makes me feel! One opens my heart, another gives me a sense of freedom or calm or joy…

While you're free to explore this book the way you want, I wish you also pay attention to how each image makes YOU feel… and reflect on the insights I shared with you. A few images don't have any text—it is intentional, to allow you to experience some of these paintings all by yourself.

These concepts and insights helped me many times since, they're like guiding stars through my life journey.

If one day, for example, I wake up feeling that I don't have enough energy… I reconnect with *The Four Elements* to see which one is missing. Then I bring more of its energy into my life. Sometimes I even do a short meditation to reconnect with all the four elements. I just imagine myself immersed in each of them, one at a time, and notice how it feels.

When I feel that I'm going in the right direction but results are not showing up yet, instead of getting discouraged and losing my motivation… I reconnect with *The Three Levels of Reality* as a reminder to keep going, since it takes a while until I see the results in the material world. This concept helped me to break through a tough financial situation after losing a job.

These spiritual concepts helped me along the way: getting out of the debt, boosting my confidence, giving me courage to live my life with integrity, and getting curious what else life has in store for me.

It's been a great journey so far!

I hope these concepts and insights will help you too.

INGREDIENTS OF HAPPINESS

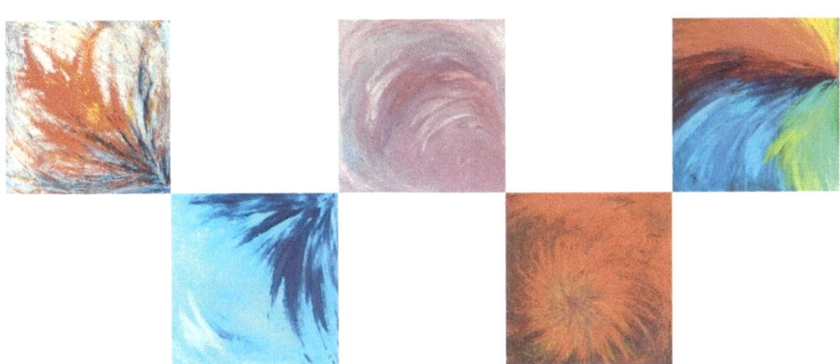

1

LOVE

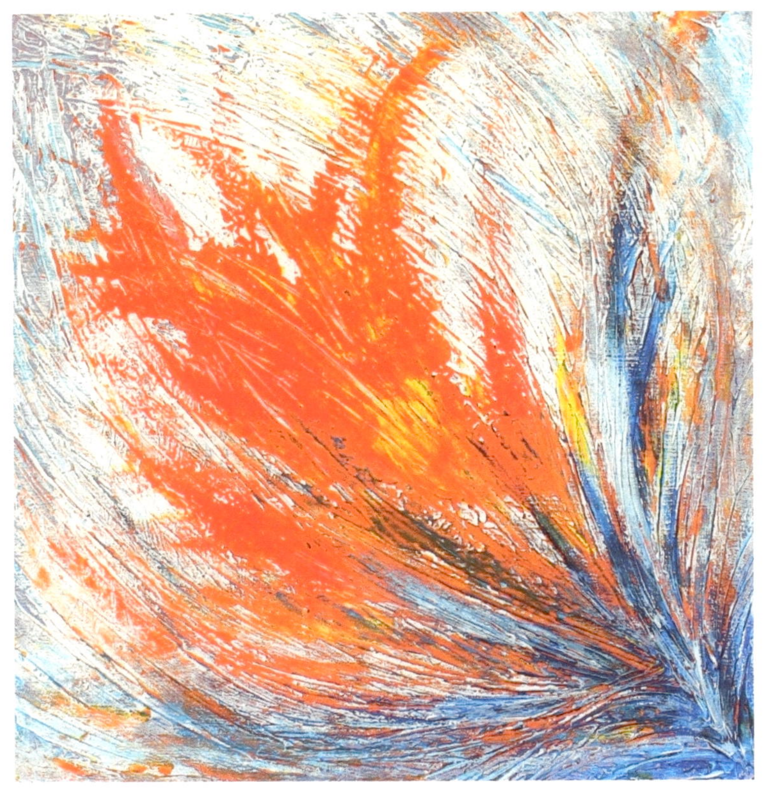

Love yourself, don't expect love only from others! This way you'll find that happiness comes from within, and it doesn't depend on others.

2

RESPECT

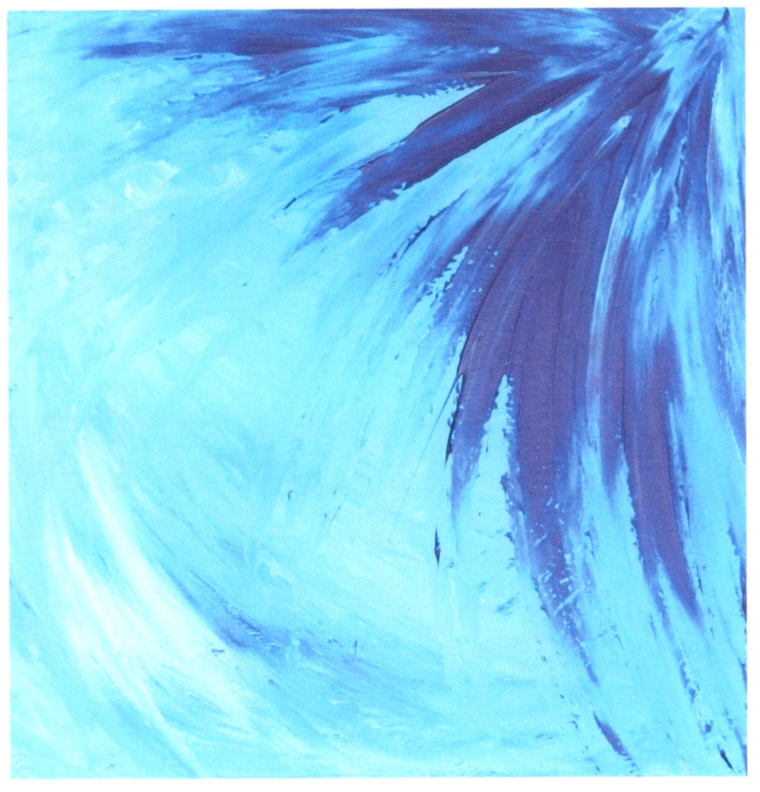

Respect others and yourself. Your opinions matter, your dreams are important and deserve your attention as well.

PEACE

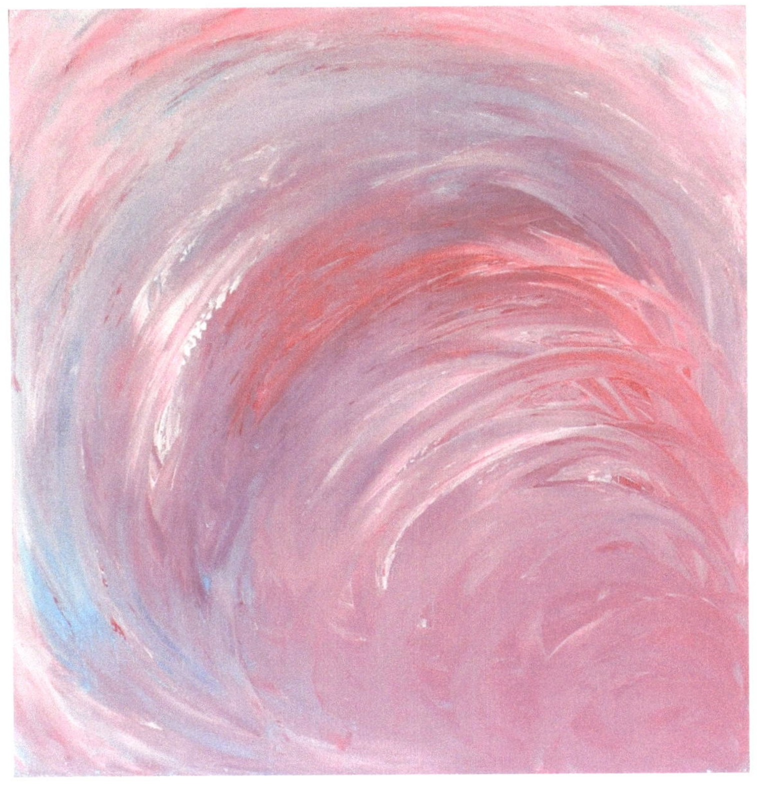

Make **Peace** with yourself. No matter what you did in the past, you can do better from now on.

GRATITUDE

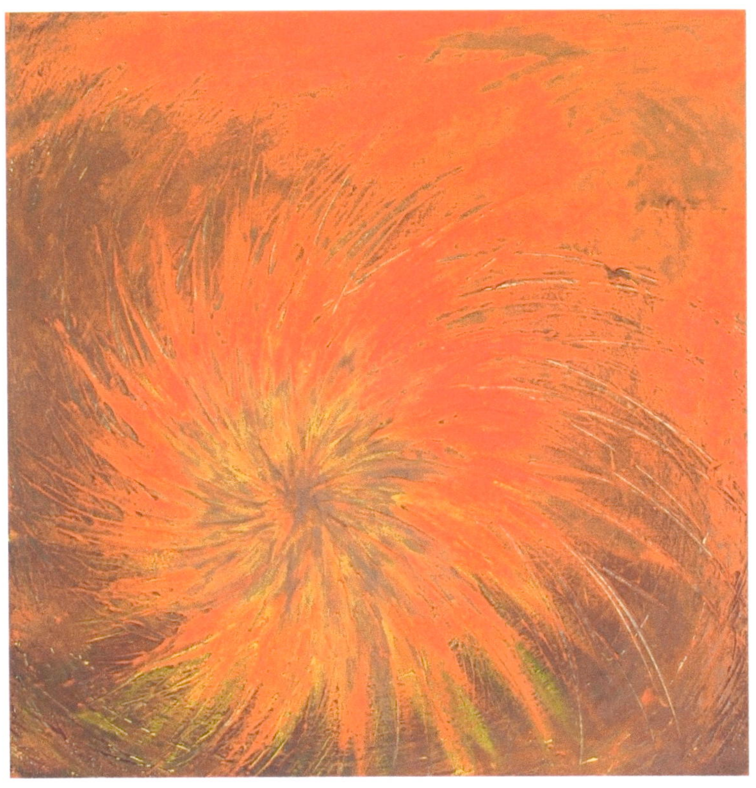

Express **Gratitude**, even if you don't fully understand why and what's happening. Everything happens for a reason. You'll understand it later, if not now.

5

———

ONENESS

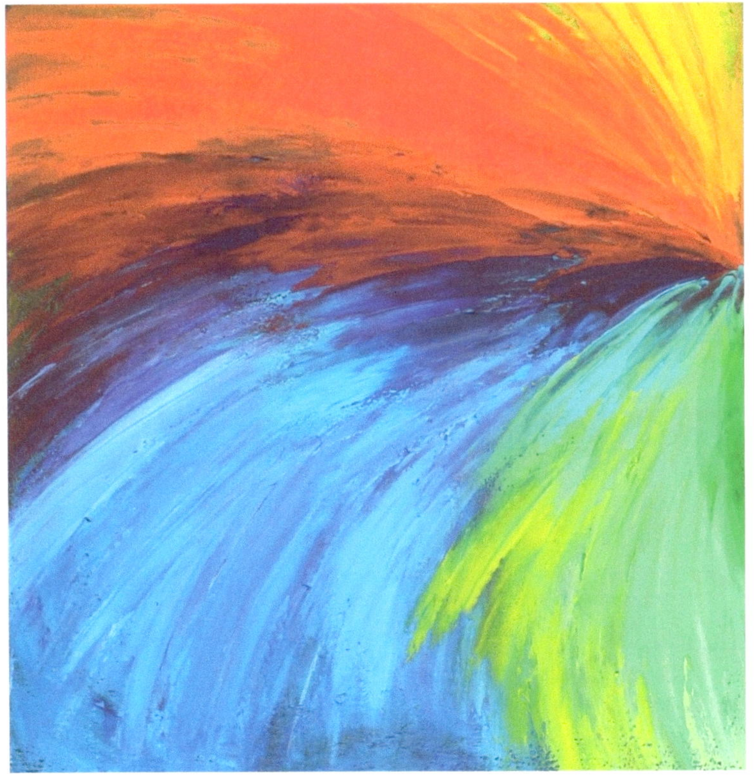

Remember you're part of **Oneness**, so you're never alone… even if it might feel that way sometimes. When it does, reach out to others and you'll feel the connectedness again.

FEMININE AND MASCULINE ENERGY

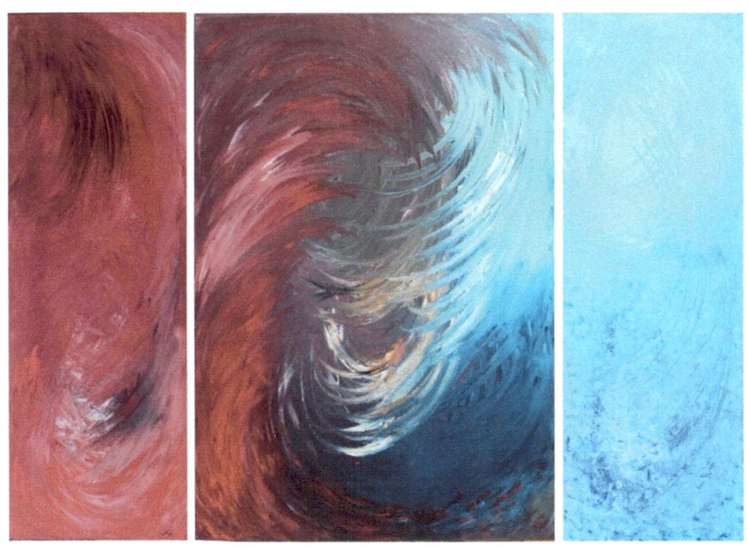

FEMININE

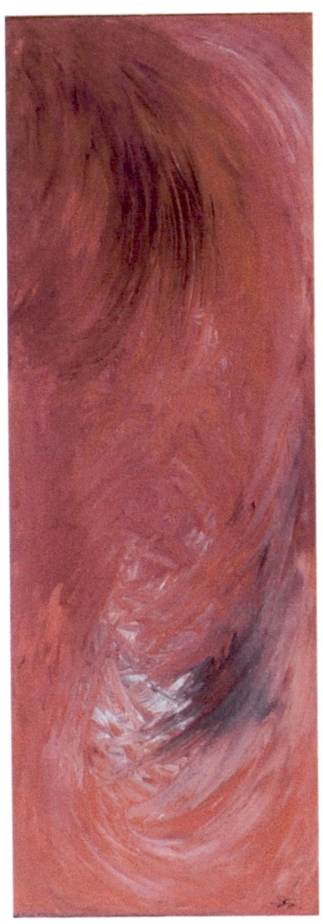

Feminine energy
is receptive, emotional,
passionate,
collaborative…

It is not necessarily
gender specific.

MASCULINE

Masculine energy is assertive, rational, competitive, determined…

It is not necessarily gender specific.

THE DANCE

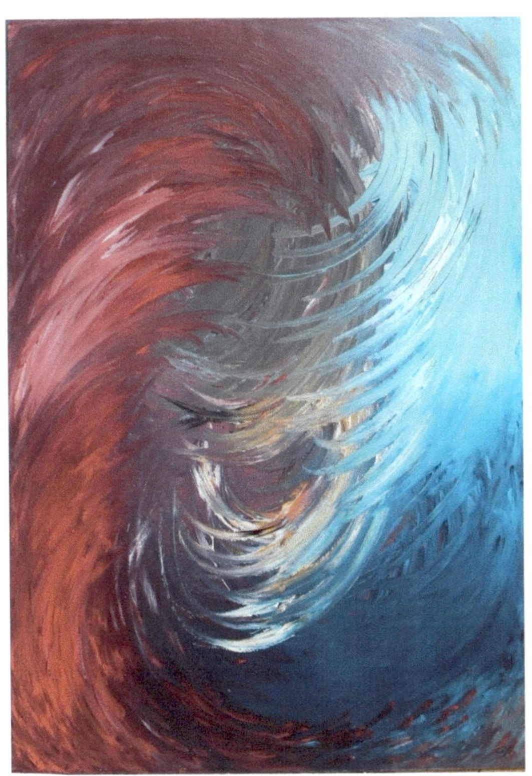

The **dance** back and forth between the **Masculine** and **Feminine** energies, within each of us, creates a more enjoyable and fulfilling life— with positive effects on the entire world.

THE FOUR ELEMENTS

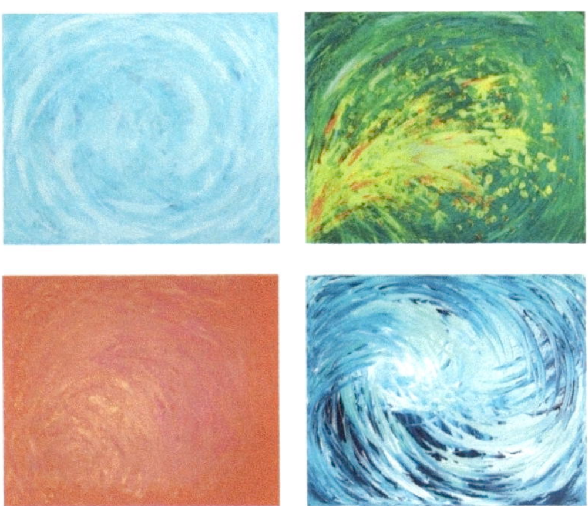

1

AIR

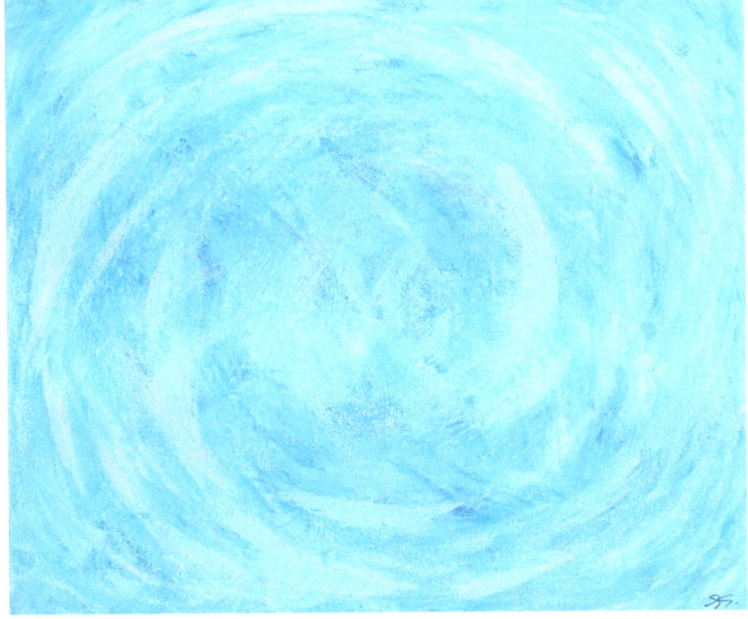

Air is the mind's ability to perceive and express—especially related to personal interactions—thought forms and abstract ideas. If missing in your life: bring in more *Air* energy, practice deep breathing, meditation.

2
───

EARTH

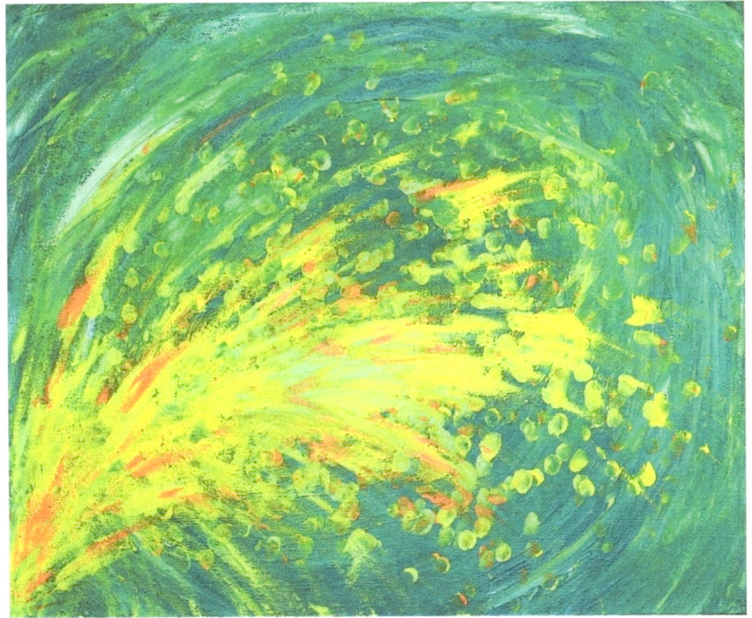

Earth is attunement to the world of physical forms, and the practical ability to utilize and improve the material world. If missing in your life: look for ways to connect more with *Earth* energy—grounding, connecting with nature.

WATER

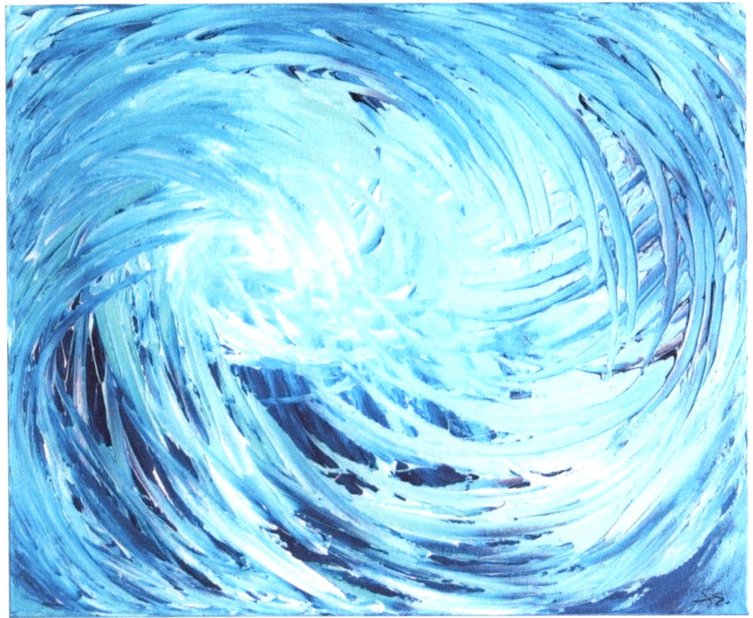

Water is cooling, going with the flow, feeling responsive, empathy. If missing in your life: reconnect with *Water* energy —visualize diving in a deep body of water or sitting in a middle of a waterfall.

FIRE

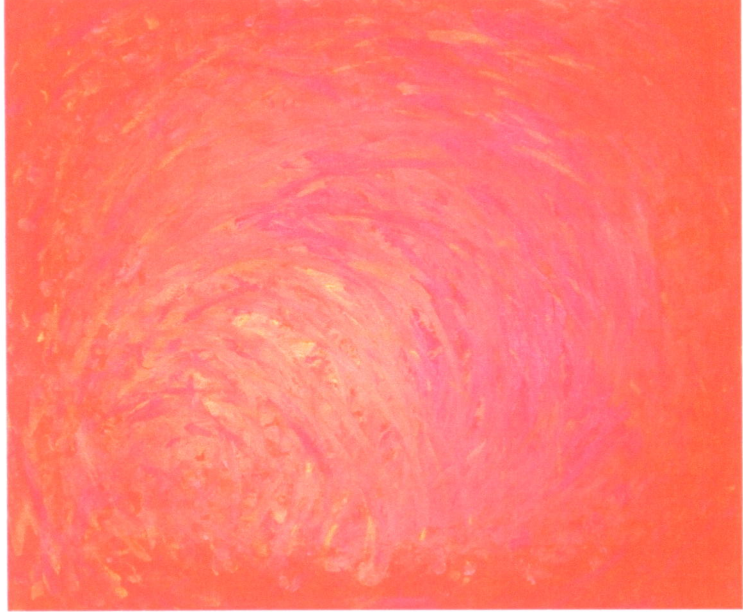

Fire is enthusiasm, faith, encouragement, and drive to express yourself. If missing in your life: find ways to bring more *Fire* energy into your life—connect with a cause dear to your heart, do things that you love to do or you resonate with.

BEFORE AND AFTER

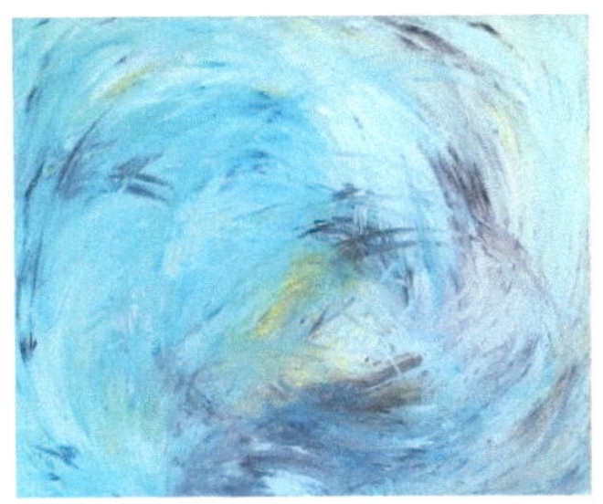

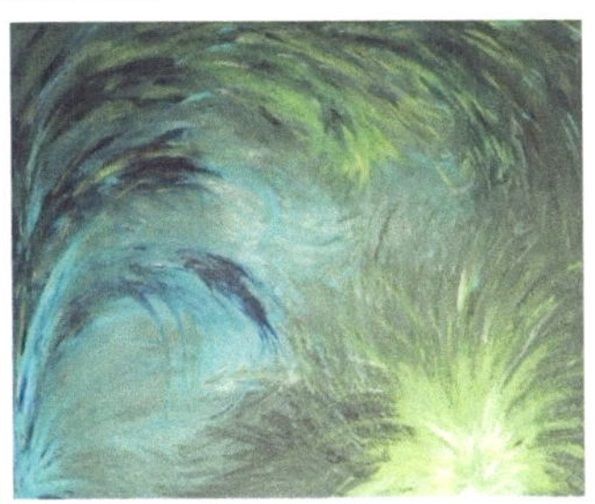

1

BEFORE OPENING UP

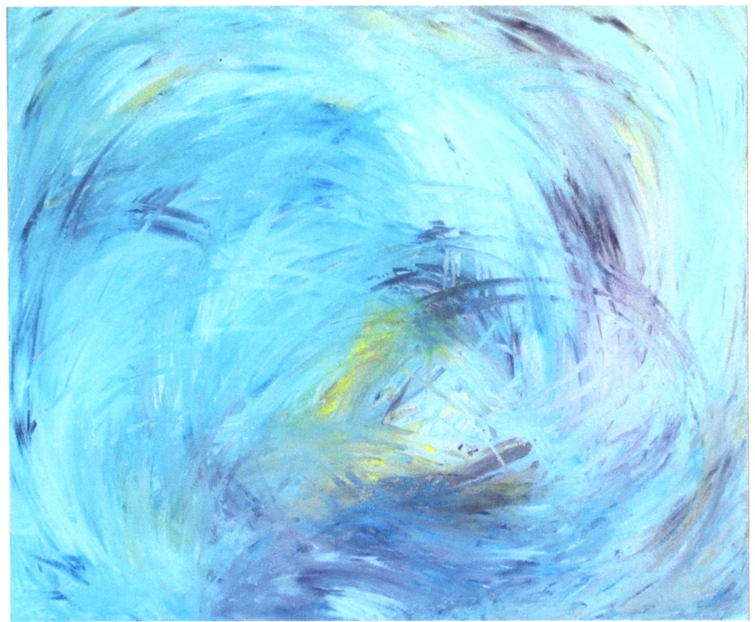

There is a tension accumulating inside when we don't speak up for ourselves. It might go unnoticed for a while, but it destroys gradually the connection with whom we really are— until we don't know anymore!

AFTER

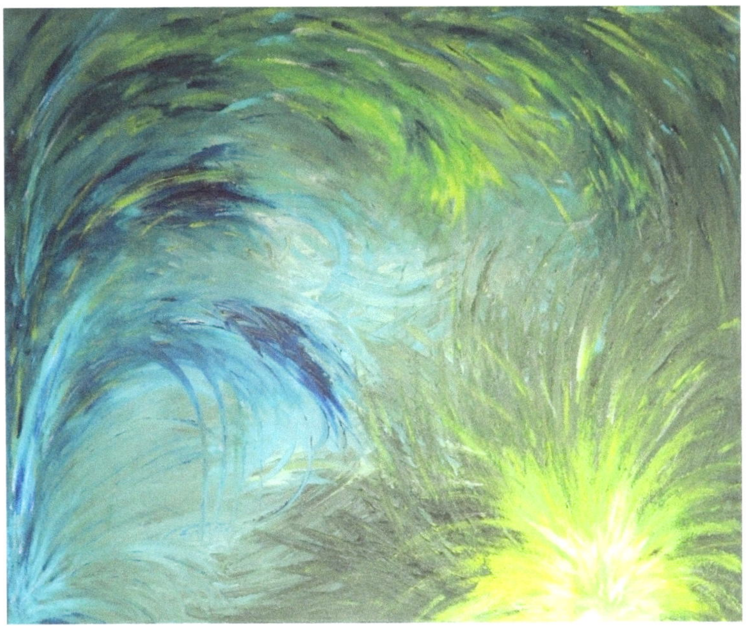

There is a powerful force unleashed when we do open up and express ourselves, giving birth to new opportunities for living life to its fullest.

THREE LEVELS OF REALITY

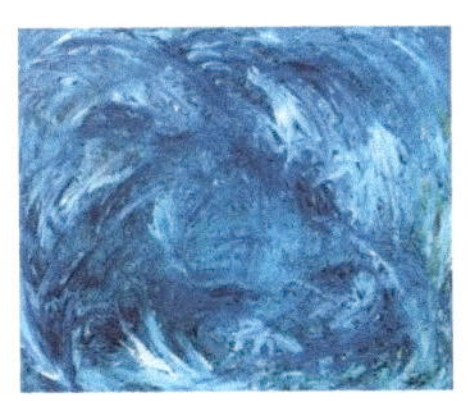

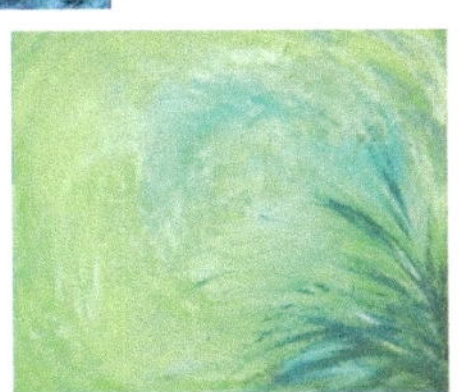

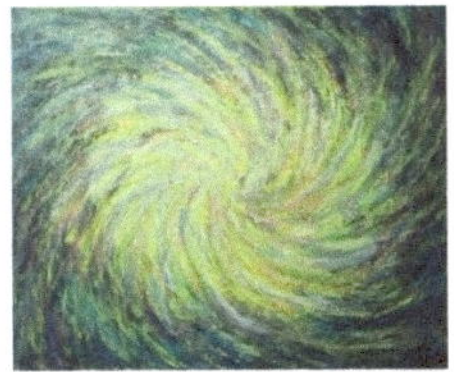

1
———

POTENTIALITY LEVEL

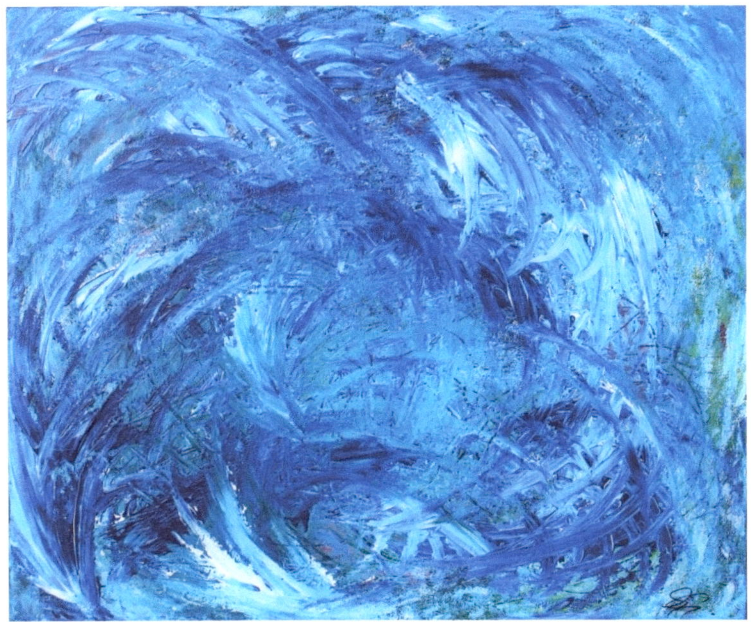

Potentiality Level brings forth a great idea to catch and fly with, for a better life journey. We connect unintentionally with this field, in those moments when the mind is quiet—allowing life itself to *spea*k to us, giving directions on how to build our *Path of the Heart*.

DREAMING LEVEL

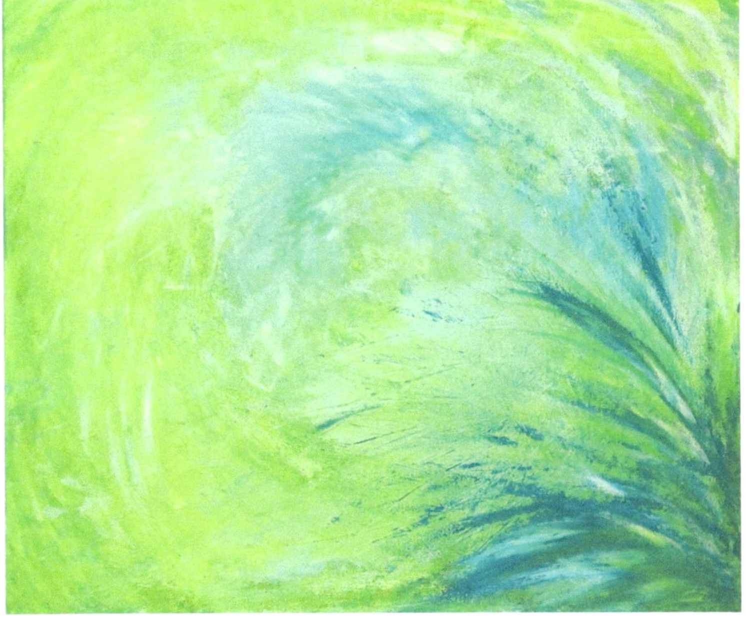

Dreaming Level—thinking often about that idea—brings to the surface positive energy and motivation. It's time to set an intention, and take the right actions toward achieving it (even when the results are not visible yet).

3

CONSENSUS REALITY

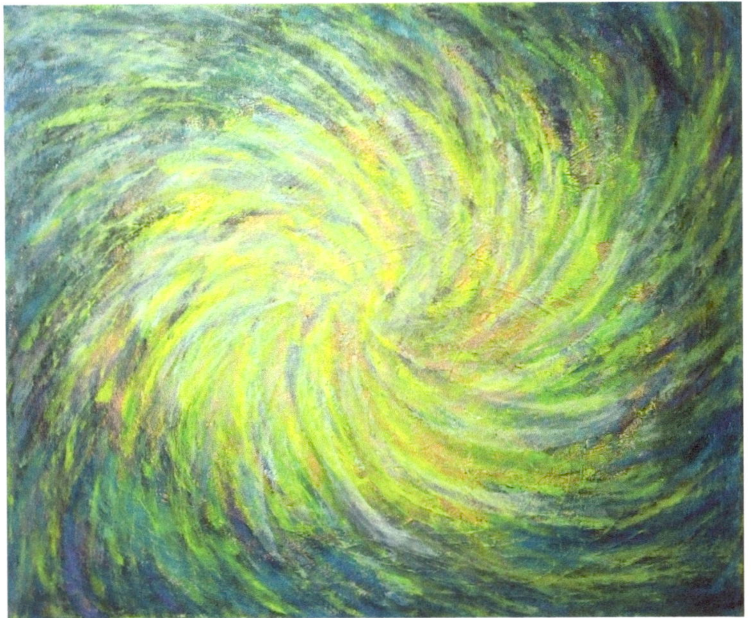

Consensus Reality is the playground where our ideas manifest, the place where everyone can see the results. Without actions taken consistently and proper attitude while in the *Dreaming Level,* our ideas might not manifests in *Consensus Reality.*

VIBRATIONS

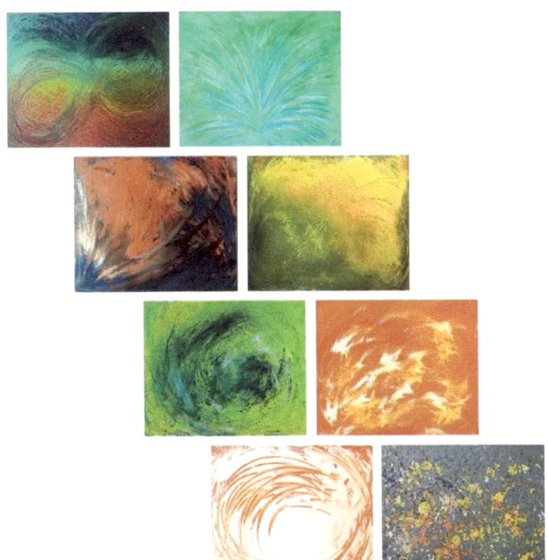

1

BEING IN THE NOW

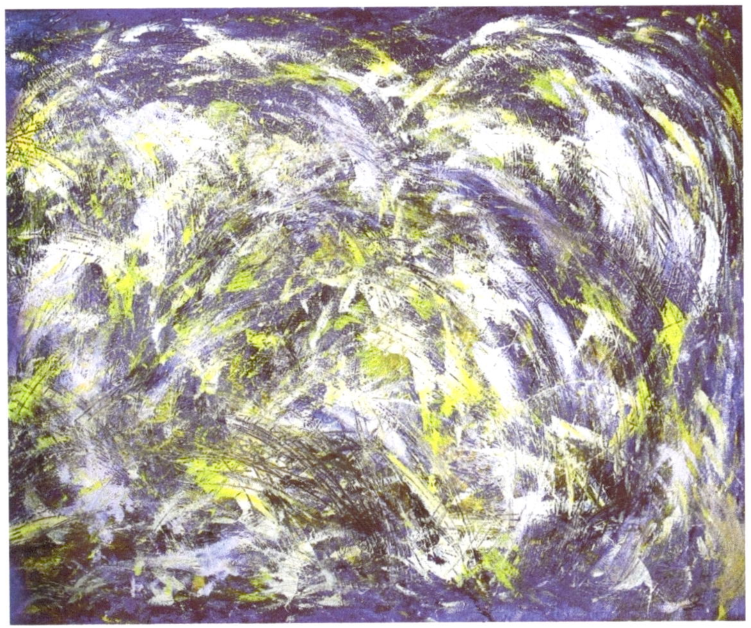

Being in the Now is about awakening our senses, paying attention to the present moment—instead of rethinking the past, guessing the future, judging or analyzing.

2

———

GOING THROUGH THE STORM
POWERED BY INNER POWER

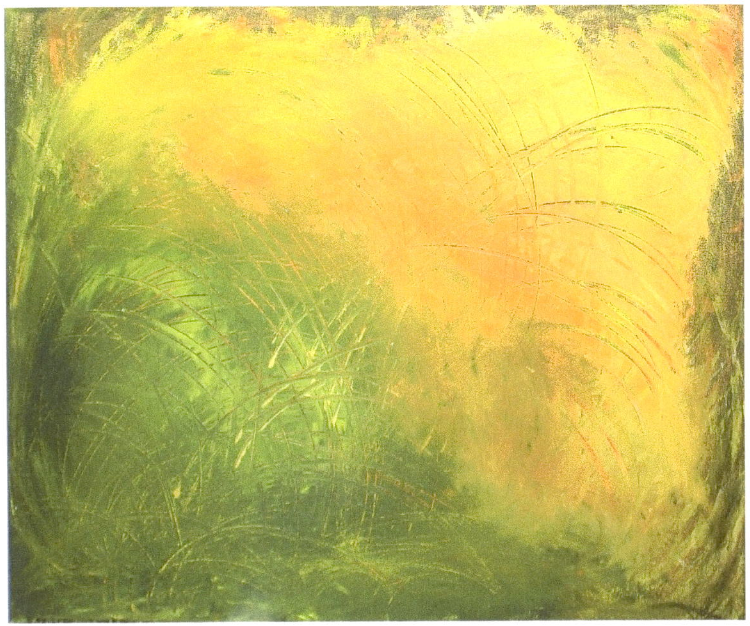

Going through the "storm" (difficult times) is enhancing our resilience and creativity—if we rely more on our inner power than on external help.

SPRING TIME

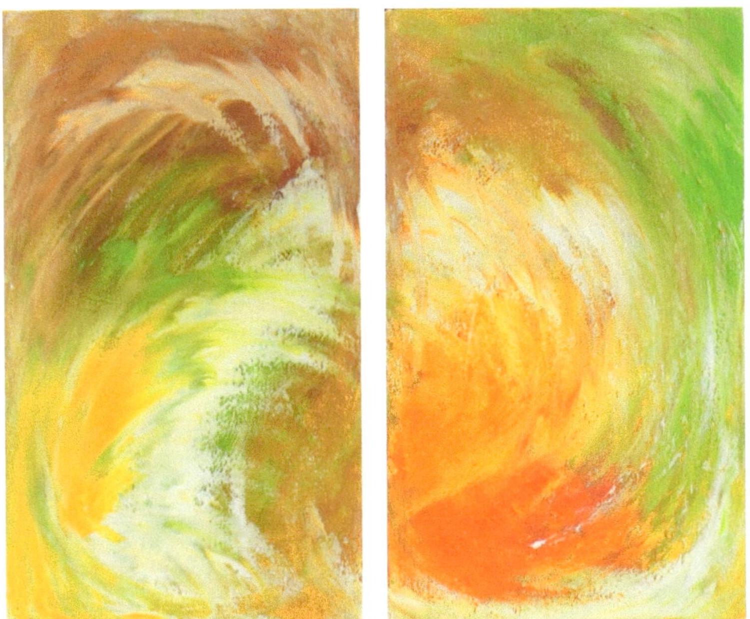

Like seasons, life also has cycles—ups and downs—but it is never the same since we can learn from, and build on previous experiences. **Spring Time** is about new beginnings.

WEALTH

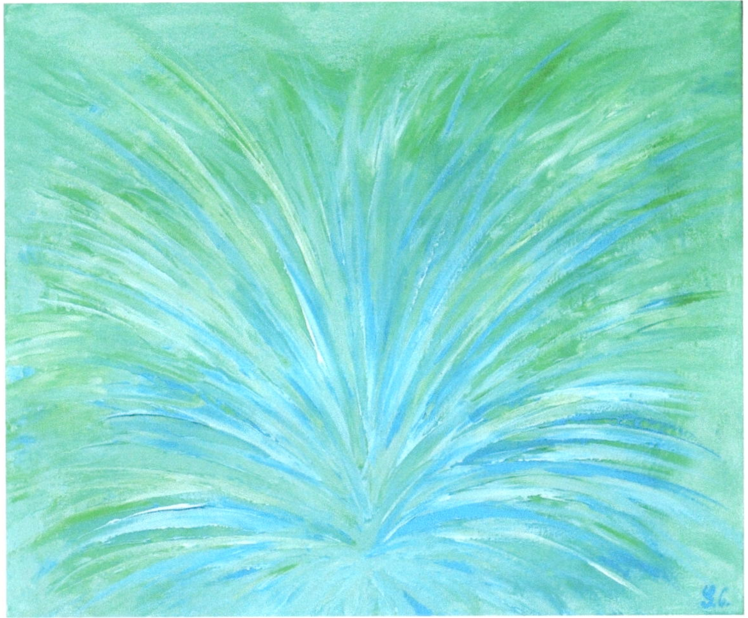

Wealth is a state of being. It is about acknowledging and accepting what life brings us, and taking the responsibility to tap into our talents to build a better world for all of us.

5
———

ABUNDANCE

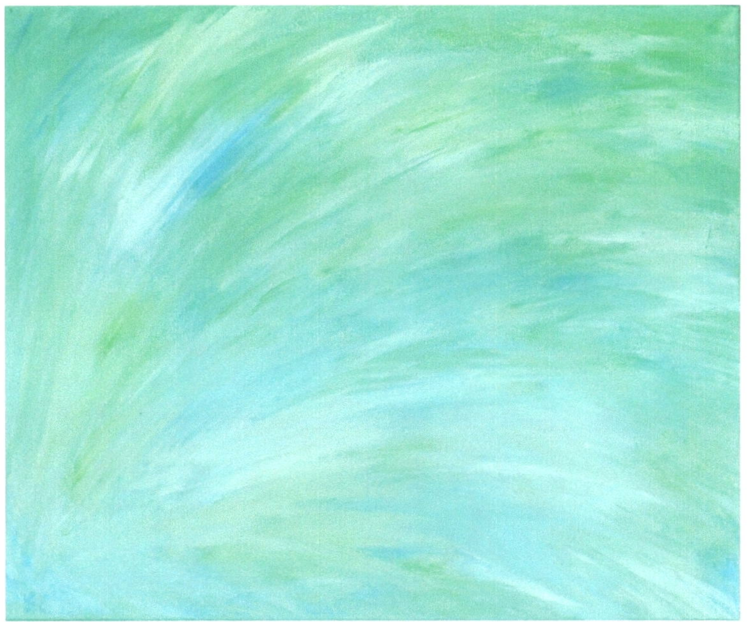

Abundance comes with expanding our awareness and allowing the flow of life to take us on a journey. Not from limiting ourselves through fears, negative emotions and limiting beliefs.

HEALTH

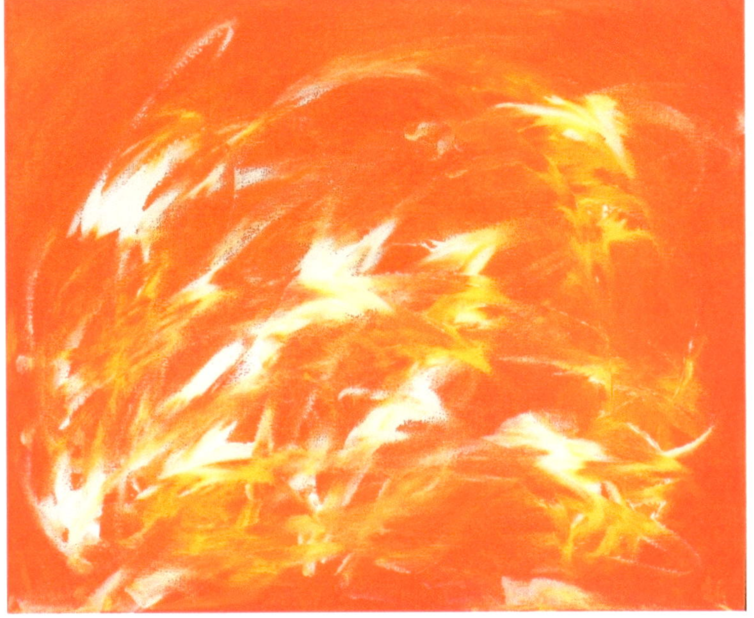

Health comes from the freedom of being yourself, open to the others' ideas, giving yourself permission to…

ATTRACT POSITIVITY

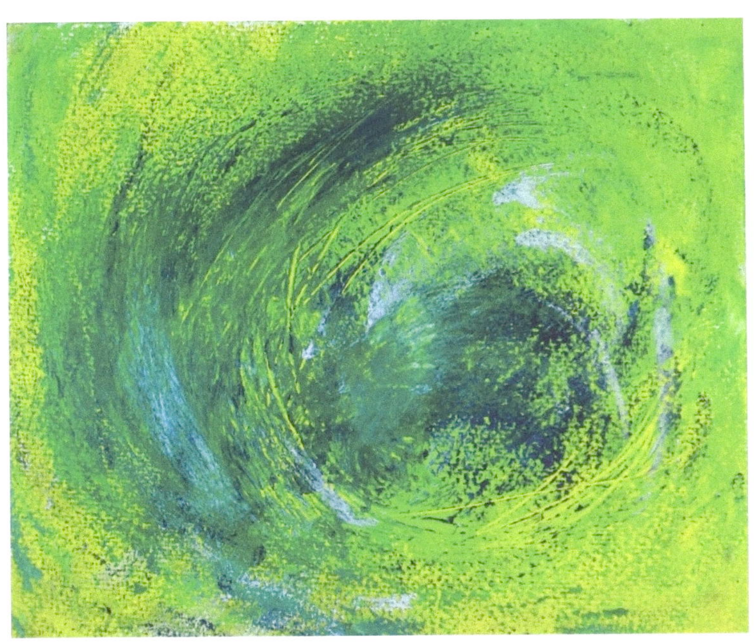

8

PROVIDING VALUE

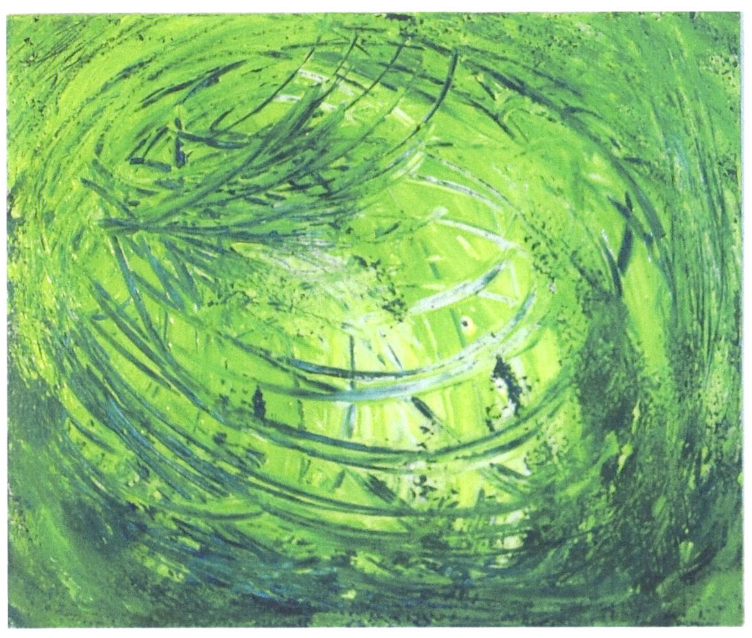

TRUSTING THE UNIVERSE

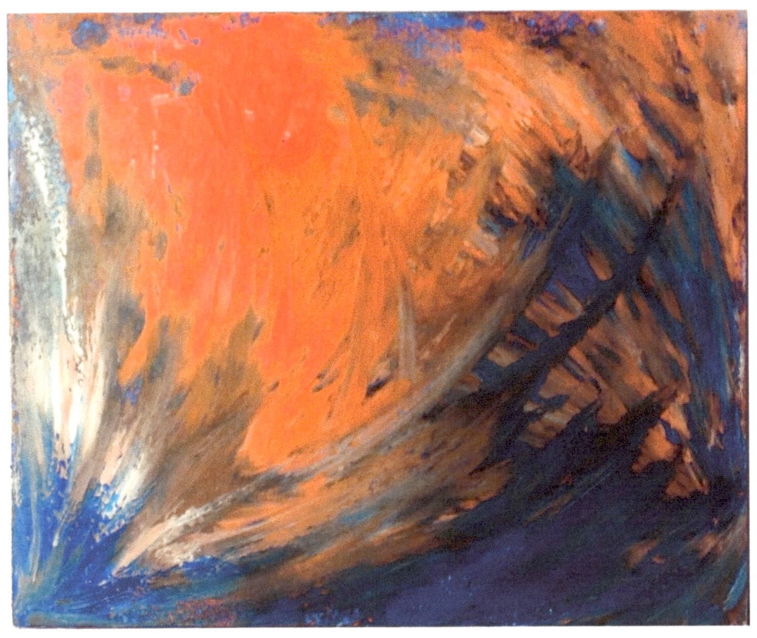

ENTHUSIASM

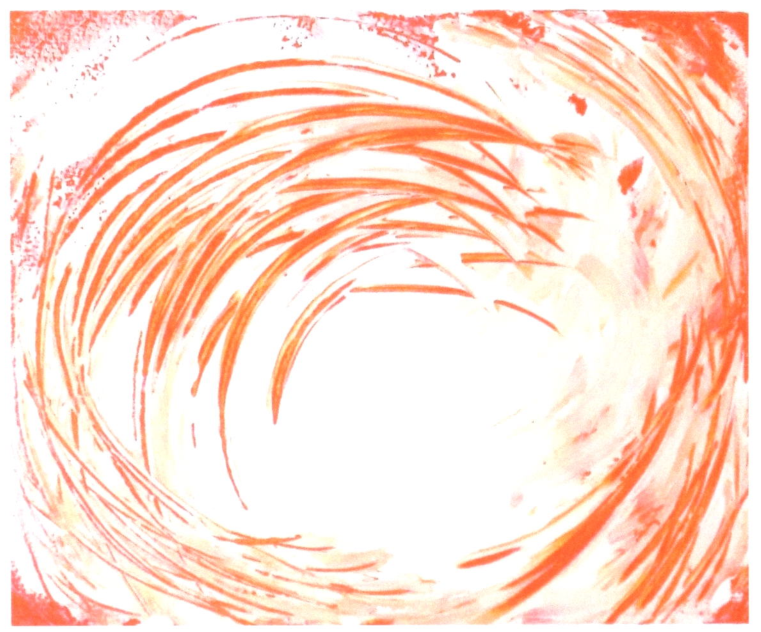

FREEDOM

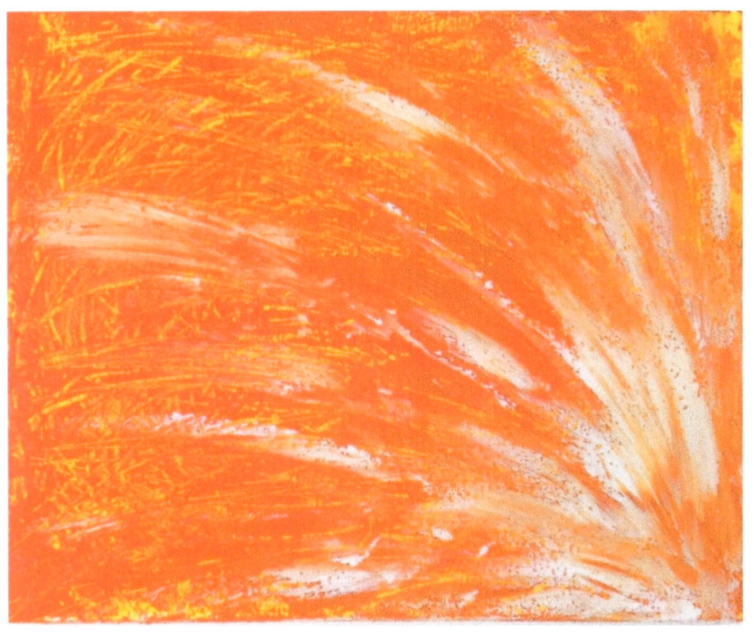

SPIRITUALITY

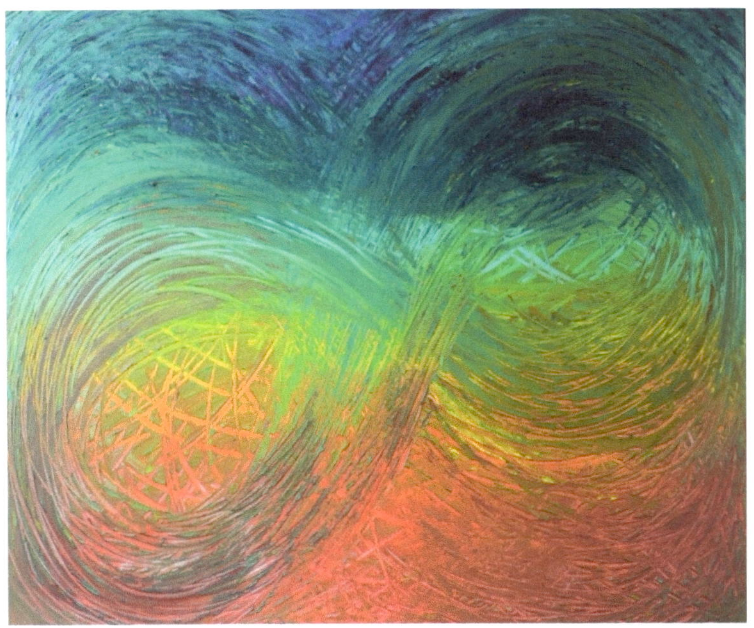

Everything is energy, flowing in and out, connecting with higher and lower realms in an infinite dance. **Spirituality** recognizes the perpetual movement of energy, evolving from one state to another, taking each of us on a unique journey.

13
———

BEYOND

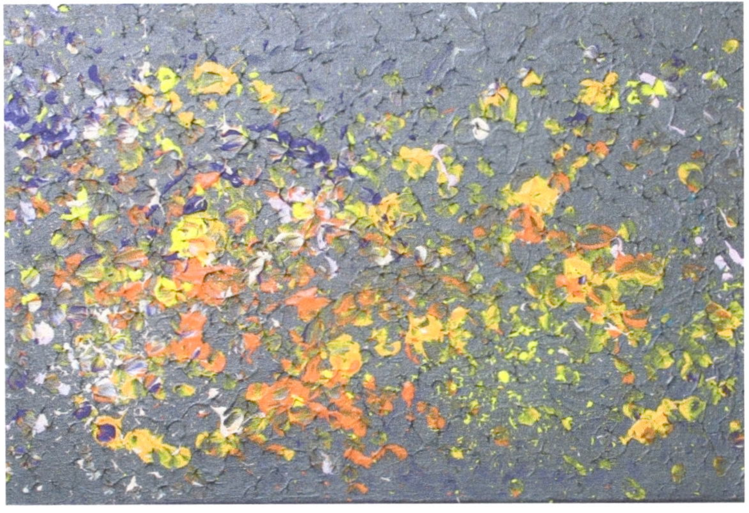

Beyond the veil of what we call *reality* is a playful creative energy, willing to express itself and expand our perception. Don't fool yourself that what you see, hear, or learn is every-thing. Be open to explore, create, and expand your limits…

NOW YOUR TURN!

I'm curious:

• What did you resonate with from this book?
• Did you get caught in the visuals or also notice how they made you feel?
• What did you learn for yourself and will apply in your life?

As you probably know, browsing a book like this—or reading any book actually—is not enough. While our conscious mind might learn new concepts or is reminded of others, none of this will automatically improve our lives. Soon we get back to our routines, forgetting these concepts... unless we put systems in place to remind ourselves to take repeated action, until they're fully integrated... so they become a second nature. And that takes practice and perseverance!

For example, when I first learned *The Three Levels of Reality* concept in my Organization and Relationship Systems Coaching (ORSC™) training, it blew my mind how simple and powerful this concept is. So I drew two lines on a big paper, and named the three blank spaces *Essence Level, Dreaming Level,* and *Consensus Reality.* Then I taped that paper on a door I was going through often in my home, as a daily reminder to apply this concept in everything I do. I painted the triptych *The Three Levels of Reality* later, for a solo painting exhibition, renaming *Essence Level* as *Potentiality Level*—it made more sense to me.

I described *The Three Levels of Reality* process in more details in this blog post, accompanied by a free ebook:
GabrielaCasineanu.com/3-levels-reality-process/

I strongly believe that everything is energy, vibrating at different levels, and such visual representations could act as reminders to bring more wisdom and positivity into our lives.

That is my wish for you too!

~ Gabriela

ABOUT THE AUTHOR

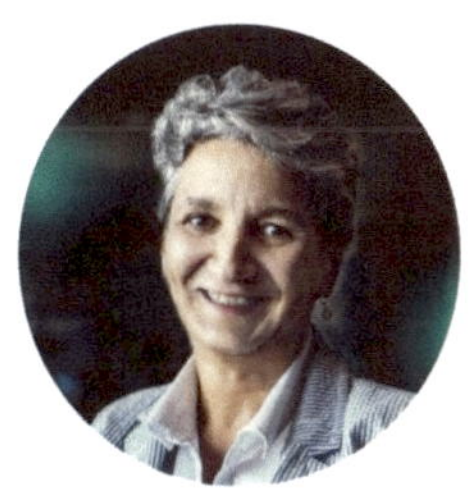

Award-winning author and professional coach, Gabriela Casineanu has successfully overcome several life challenges and career transitions.

She started her professional path in electronic engineering, then added entrepreneurship, coaching, artistic expressions, and writing... continuing to explore life with the curiosity of a child!

With a daily meditation practice and a passion for personal growth, nature and outdoor activities, Gabriela relies on intuition to guide her next steps. She writes books that she would have liked to read to help her navigate life more easily.

More about Gabriela, her books, and to receive updates:
GabrielaCasineanu.com

ALSO BY GABRIELA CASINEANU

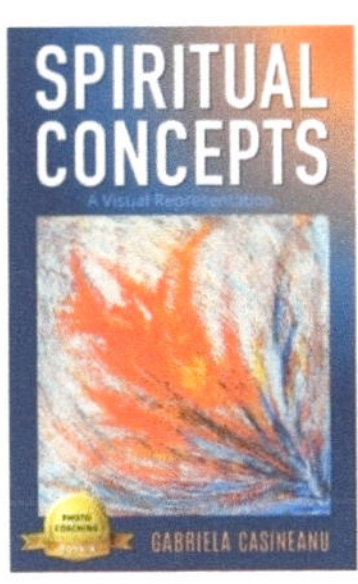

Please leave a review for
SPIRITUAL CONCEPTS: A VISUAL REPRESENTATION
to help others understand what the book is about.

BOOKS

List of books: GabrielaCasineanu.com/book

Introvert Strengths series

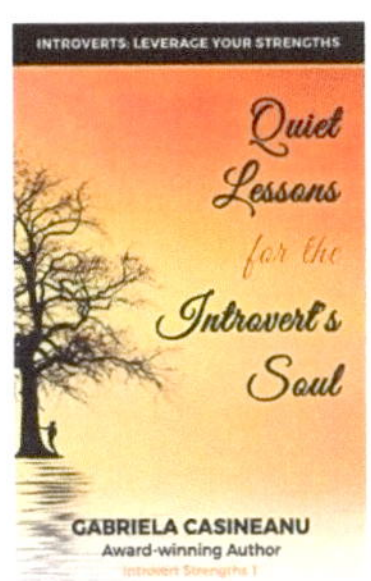
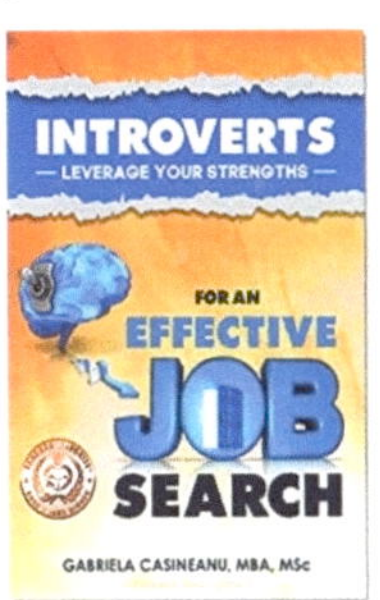

Job Search/Career series

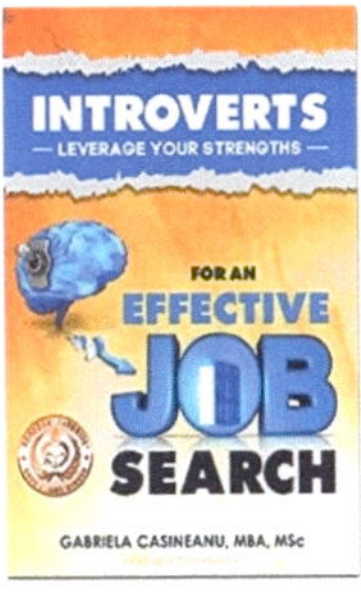
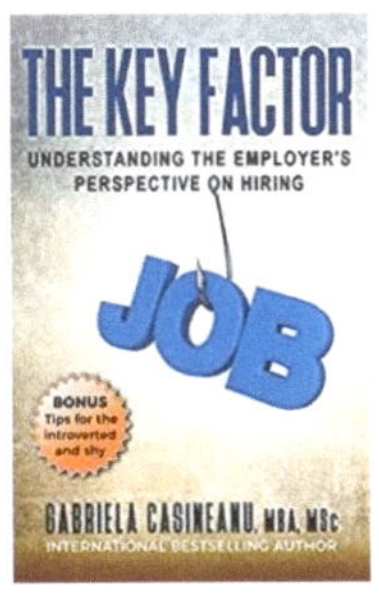
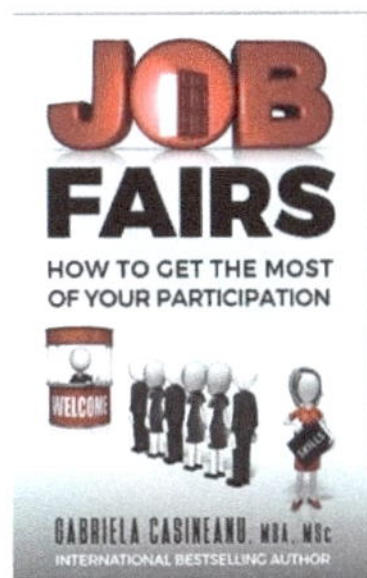

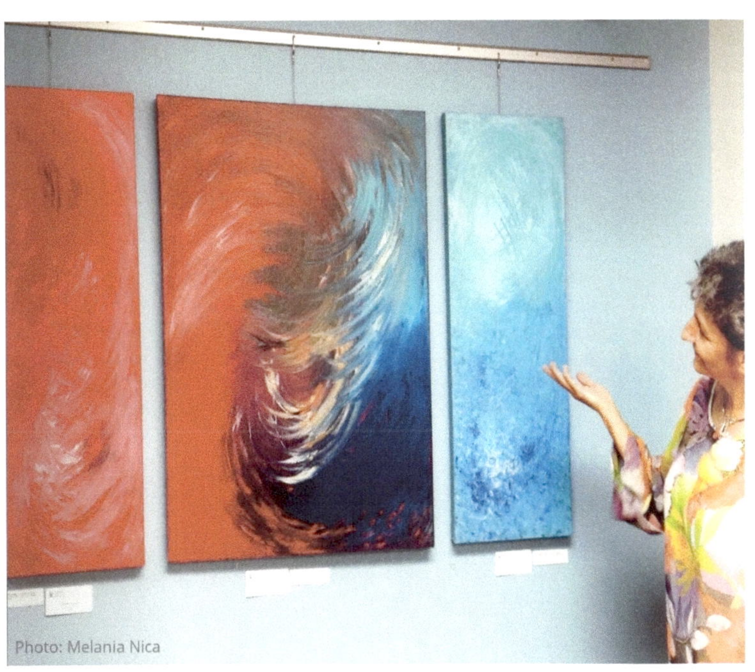

Thank you!
~ Gabriela Casineanu